Rise.Rose.Risen

Iris Rose

Printed in the United States of America
ISBN: Softcover   978-1-969213-14-4
           e-Book   978-1-969213-15-1
Republished by: TwinVerse Prime
Publication Date: 09/01/2025

To buy a copy of this book, please contact:
Iris Rose
iris.rose.poems.90@gmail.com

Roses are red.
Violets are blue.
When flowers die,
They turn ugly too.

CONTENTS

The higher you climb, the farther you might fall, and yet the closer you may be to touching the sun.

Here Comes the Sun

Once, there was a man called Ray, and Ray had a small yet unreachable dream from the day he was born--he wanted to live in the light. You see, Ray lives in Darkness, a patch of land where the sun never shines and the sky is covered with tall, towering mountains that no one could ever climb. And so, Ray lived in a never-ending twilight where no sun, no moon, and no stars guided his way.

To everyone, Ray had a strange dream. Often, they could catch him looking up into the sky, chasing what little light he could see. They told him that things had always been so dim and never ever would they change. But instead of keeping his head down and living each day unquestioningly, he went on each day searching for a way to see the light in its full majestic beauty. That is how Ray's story begins.

I Am. I Was. I Will

I am hiding.
Hiding from the world, lest it see my fear and use it against me.

I am recovering.
Recovering from a wound so deep, it has taken years and years to close up.

I am comfortable.
Comfortable in my solitude, I dare not step out of my protective little bubble.

I am watching.
Watching as the world passes me by, only slightly aware that I'm falling behind.

I was ahead.
Ahead of the race that society has asked me to run.

I was ahead.
Ahead of myself when I thought I could do it all because I clearly could not.

I was happy.
Happy with my accomplishments until someone rudely told me I'd done nothing of note.

I was failing.
Failing to realize that my life was a failure in others' eyes.

I will keep going.
Keep going because there simply isn't anywhere else to go but forward.

I will keep failing.
Keep failing because I am battered and bruised and have lost much of my will to fight.

I will keep fighting.
Keep fighting with what I have left in me because I am alive.

I Hear Voices

This voice in my head tells me everything wrong with me.
And I listen to it all too often.
In my every fall, its laugh echoes,
In my every flaw, its bravado strengthens.
Every day, it says, "Give up and let go."
And my head pounds every time I resist.

Whenever it speaks, this voice, it gets louder and louder.
And now, it is my unwelcome guest.
It lives in me, coaxing me, never wavering,
Pushing me to the brink of hysteria.
Every day, like a mantra, "You deserve this."
And my mouth moves, answering its every attack.

Why resist, I wonder.
I believe the voice wholeheartedly.
When it speaks, I listen.
When it beckons, I respond.
I am small. I am insignificant. Why resist?

Once Upon a Time

Once upon a time, the miles we needed to walk didn't matter.
Hand in hand, you and I were ready to face anything.
You promised you'd always walk those miles with me,
Yet here I am, walking alone, unable to see an arm's length ahead.

Once upon a time, our laughter echoed through the night.
We found the brighter side of every shadowed corner.
You swore you'd find even the smallest sliver of light with me,
But now I stumble and fall, searching for your outstretched hand.

Once upon a time, we dreamed of building a life together.
We believed in the love that brought us here.
You told me you'd be everything I needed you to be,
But today, my failings have proven greater than your love.

Once upon a time wasn't so long ago.
And yet, we've forgotten the vows we once held sacred.
We lost everything—and nothing, really—
Because you can't lose what was never truly yours.

Fleeting

I was in a dark place and a beam of light streaked through.
It was radiant, made the darkness less suffocating.
So instead of slicing my flesh, I ripped through the veil of darkness.
In a desperate effort to illuminate my whole being,
and see who I have become.

I was in a dark place when a beam of light gave me back my sight.
It wasn't as threatening as a flash of lighting, but as subtle as a candle burning.
So instead of spiraling into the depths of eternal sleep,
My stinging eyes remained open, drinking in that light,
and seeing exactly everything I have done.

I was in a dark place, and I stepped into the beam of light.
It gave me courage to step closer, gave me hope to keep going.
And instead of dwelling on the stumbles and falls, I got up and kept walking,
I focused on the lengths that the light let me travel,
and I saw what lay ahead of me.

And it is beautiful.
Imperfect.
With dark corners.
Certainly, never as black as the place behind me.

Time can either be a cruel mistress
or a comfortable companion.

ICE

The Cold But Pleasing Blast from the Past

She was wearing leg warmers on an impossibly hot day. I then noticed her black and red fingerless gloves that had rhinestones on it.

Truthfully, she looked like she stepped straight out of a cool manga, slightly unreal in the cacophony of sounds made by strangers trapped in a steel, moving thing with wheels.

She had long, straight, jet-black hair. Her school uniform was hidden beneath a black trench coat and obscured a school ID that was covered in anime stickers. She was beautiful, very similar to someone I used to know. Best of all, she was reading a copy of one of Rick Riordan's many mythology books.

As I observed her, engrossed in the book, I thought, I bet she's slightly eccentric and incredibly smart, much like her.

I was compelled to talk to her, but I didn't. Creepy old lady wasn't something I wanted to be identified as. But how she reminded me of the carefree life. She reminded me of the time I wanted to go back to so desperately. Obviously, I didn't react impulsively, so I looked on with just a hint of envy for her youth, for her lack of care in a harsh world. She was happily enveloped in the world of pretend monsters, of quirky teenagers going on world-saving adventures that always ended well.

I tried to imagine the thoughts in her head, until my stop came into view, and I silently bid goodbye to the personification of how life used to be and shall never be again.

Where Are You Now, Dear Ones

Where are you now, dear ones?
Do you still tell people you're twenty-two?
Where are the moments of unbothered laughter?
How are the bodies that could shrink at will?
Did we really believe we could hide behind potted plants?

Why could we get away with life
with only the spare change in our pockets
and the sheer will to eat?
How could we have gotten out unscathed?
And yet, how could we have not?

The lives we lived, filled with promise,
the hope we had, enough to cross oceans,
and such confidence to look ahead unjaded.
We were ready to take on the world,
And who's to say we haven't?
After all, we're still living legends.

Moments and Memories

The best years of your life happened a decade ago.
And here you are, pining over them.
You will yourself to feel the way you used to.
You felt unstoppable, didn't you?
Everything you wanted was within reach.
Everything was a constant rush.
But now, those moments are reduced to faded memories.
A photo, frozen in time.
A date that passes.
Year by year, you wonder the same thing.
Where did all the chances go?
How did all your bravado fade?
Why did you stop the adventure?
When did you become just another memory?
Moments. You're left with moments.
And you resign yourself to saying or thinking or writing,
"This was who I used to be."
Sure. Sure of who I was and what I wanted.

Hello, Little Girl

This one girl said to the other,
This is how you used to be.

You used to have much more than you could handle.
Year after year, filled with accomplishment, travel, and
meaningful conversation.

You used to love the life you now deign to live.
Close your eyes and picture it, the hope and the anticipation to
show the world what you're made of.

You used to say that everything would work out.
That you're strong and you could handle anything that anyone
threw at you.

You used to, so why can't you now?

The other girl responded,
This is how I am.
Broken but never beyond repair and still able to function.

I have much more than I can handle.
Responsibility, accountability, and tough decisions day after day
after day.

I deign to awake to the same life I have since lived.
I close my eyes and wish to do much more than I already am.

I believe, still, that everything can work out.
I am strong but I do not need to handle everything that anyone throws at me.

I used to be that, chasing the next biggest adventure.
Now I am this, knowing that the biggest adventure is conquering far beyond who you used to be and living to tell your tale.

Underneath These Thick Curls

I hear your voice sometimes, your mantra echoes in my head.
You'd tell me of the dreams you had for me,
the woman I would become, and the life I would live.
In your mind, I was brilliant,
but I never could live up to the brilliance only you could see.

I picture the days we spent sometimes; your face etched in my
memories.
You'd sit me on your knee, asking about my day,
what I thought of growing up to be a lawyer or a businesswoman.
To you, I could make it,
but I never did make it as far as you hoped.

I'd sit shotgun sometimes, your driving always a comfort to me.
You'd take me to the pier to get shipments,
to show me the future you worked so hard to build.
If it had been up to you, I'd be driving my own car now,
but I never even did learn to ride the bike.

I never got to see my day in court,
and I don't talk as much as I used to.
I'm not as brave as I once was,
and perhaps I have lost some of the shine you saw.
I work an ordinary 9–5, just like everyone else,
but I stand on my own two feet, mostly with my head held high.

I am your unruly, curly hair and your beautiful lashes.
Sometimes I speak with the words you engraved in my head.
But most of all, I am your legacy,
and I hope to God you're happy with who I've turned out to be.

Aphrodite is beautiful but Eros'
arrows strike without mercy.

Who I Am to You

She was at one of their annual family dinners. The laughter at the dinner table seemed infectious. There was music drifting through the air. She smiles, because that's what's expected of her. She looks over to him, cracking a joke that barely registers in her head. She laughs along, tilting her head back and putting her hand in her mouth to hide the sobs that escaped her lips.

Her fingers tighten around the stem of the glass. It's exhausting but she plays her part well. She will be whoever he needs her to be right now. If he wants her to be lighthearted, calm, and unbothered, that's who she is. If he needs her to listen, she listens. She knows just how to turn on the quirky, fun, and submissive person she's playing right now, especially when it'll get him to save face.

For a moment, she excuses herself, goes to the farthest corner of the house, closes the door, and lets the tears fall. *Just one moment.* That's all she needs.

A lady never laughs too loud, never cries in public, always behaves the right way. Her grandma's voice echoes in her head. Yes, she's spent years being exactly who everyone she ever loves needs her to be. So, today, she does the same. She takes a deep breath, fixes herself, and goes back out again.

Against Reason

When once you held my hand, I felt giddy.
And whenever you smile at me, my heart melts.
Your laugh makes me smile,
And your voice is something of a mystery to me.

The first thing I do is scan the room for you.
And the last thing is wonder if you look for me too.
Whenever our eyes meet, I just can't help it.
I am captured by your strange goofy look.

You're not charming, nor are you a prince.
You're no Jack to my Rose,
And you don't seem like my type at all.
But you've got my attention.

Euphoria

You looked at me, and I went to Heaven.
You stared straight into my soul,
And saw me beautiful.

You spoke to me, and I was in euphoria.
Your mellifluous words awakened me,
With promises kept in lock and key.

You heard me, and suddenly I existed.
As though you lived for every beat of my heart,
You moved in its unsteady rhythm.

You see me, you hear me, you love me.
But you never deem yourself worthy,
And my heart breaks with your loathing.

With You, It Matters Not

I've said it once and will say it again, and again when it comes.
Betrayal is inevitable in any relationship.
Whether by choice or circumstance,
It matters not.

I've known its bitter taste,
I've felt its painful sting,
I've even let it hurt me a couple of times.
But it still, it matters not.

Love or hate or resentment is my friend.
Whoever that someone may be to you,
Love and hate and resentment are your friends too.
And knowing it matters not.

We're not islands, you and I,
Him or her or even they know it.
Because what does matter is that I know.
That I feel and it matters not that I may get betrayed.

Fragments of Us

In my little book of what ifs, you're on top of the list.
Time after time, I wonder about you and me.
Us, something that could've happened.
But it didn't and it can't.

What if I waited; what if you didn't hurt?
What if circumstances pulled us closer rather than farther?
What if I was fine with it all,
And what if you never gave up?

The love that I had for you was extraordinary.
It does not consume; it does not dominate.
It is subtle and pure and has stood the test of time,
And most of all, it will never go away.

You were the someone who made me lighter,
Despite this heavy-set frame of me and mine.
You were there to turn my tears into laughs,
Despite never being in the same address for long.

I am always thankful for you and who you are.
Because who you are is precious to me.
But you will always be my biggest what if.
And I will always be your one who got away.

I do not mean to be reduced to a phone call you make on occasion.
And I'm sure you never meant to be the shadow who haunts me.
But you are that and so am I; you and I will never be an us.
And I must be content with only the memory of you.

Explore each doorway to your soul.

Beneath the Quiet

Drip. Drip. Drip. She was baffled by the sound that disturbed her much-needed sleep. Where could that dripping be coming from, she thought, debating whether it was enough reason to crack her eyes open.

Just when she thought she could get used to the sound, she sighed and let out a frustrated cry.

"Fine!" she said aloud, opening her eyes and adjusting to the dark shadows of the room she'd been living in for the past five days.

Enid had just moved into this small, squalid room. It was close to her new job, but more importantly, it was all she could afford at the moment. This was what she thought of each time she scanned the room.

Her eyes swept over the closed bathroom door, the small kitchen counter sans a sink, and the walls opposite her. She was searching, searching for where the dripping was coming from. Then, just as she raised her head, she saw it, a pool of red on the ceiling just to the right of the bed.

"What on earth!" she said, watching the red liquid steadily dripping from the ceiling.

She was on the top floor. There were no tenants above her. She got up to find out, and then, bam!

Vessel of Madness

Look here, look here,
Oh, what a pity!
She's tried too hard,
but her palms are still empty.

She pleads to deaf ears,
and seeks the counsel of mutes.
She knows much but is foolish.
She gives much but has nothing.

Look here, and see her misery,
let her be our example.
You must make wise choices
lest you be a vessel of madness.

Look there, she runs around in circles.
She picks up broken pieces,
desperately putting them back together.
What a laughable sight!

Look and see, what a spectacle.
Her fall is spectacular.
She is our infamous lesson.
Of how young girls should be.

Look at her with mocking disdain,
dishonorable, distasteful, a disgrace
You who look with pity or detestation,
Do you truly see her?

Look here, look here,
As my eyes glaze over and I cannot think.
I am hollow and numb.
I stumble, I fail and pick up my broken pieces.
You see my futile attempts and laugh,
while I sit, and ponder with utmost clarity
that I have not strength nor desire to breathe.

Linger

I loved you for your laugh and I still hear it in these walls.
I loved you for all the hours you spent enveloped in these arms.
I loved you for your voice and the way you whisper in my ears.
I loved how vulnerable you could be with me when you would
always be fine to everyone else.

I loved standing still, looking into your eyes.
I loved being your shadow, mimicking your every move.
I loved you, for everything that you are and everything you are
not.
And if you had asked me again, I would've said that I love you
still.
But you did not.

Today, I wish that you would come and see me.
I wish to see you as I did, as I still see you.
Lingering.
Because try as I may to forget, my heart remembers.
And never in this life will I ever know why.
Perhaps I'll see you in another life, the life where I can say I
didn't just love you yesterday, but today, tomorrow and always.

Boarders

A tenant was evicted today.
His room swept clean, all traces of him wiped off.
He lived to work but lost all opportunity after all.
Today, all the bridges he'd built were burnt.

A tenant was evicted today.
He paid his dues, month after painful month.
He would trudge up the steps, tired but hopeful.
Today, everyone would call him a good tenant.

A tenant was evicted today.
He didn't even know what was coming.
He thought he'd done all he could.
But today, he could do no more.

The landlord evicted another tenant today.
Despite the price he's paid, it was time.
All us tenants go, one way or another.
How would we know when we'll be evicted too?

Think of Me Fondly

I wonder what you would say when you tell someone about me.
Would you remember me fondly, with a single tear escaping
from your eye?
Would you be kind and say something good?
Would you perhaps scowl and curse my name in anger?
Or even shake your head and sigh in confusion?

I was but a tiny speck of dust, easily flicked off anybody's
clothes.
I was nothing and no one, invisible even with my rather large
frame.
I was a hopeless dreamer who saw good in everything but never
inside me.
If I knew you, I apologize.
For I have no doubt wronged you in some way or the another.

I was insufferable, you see.
So steadfast in my beliefs but always so afraid to fail.
Choosing instead to be small and unimportant rather than tall
and obnoxious.
I had such thoughts, such grand lives living in my head,
And it saddens me that no one will hear them.

Now I only ask that you tell the truth of who I was,
light a candle and send a prayer up above.
For try and try, I did, until my very last breath.

Roses come in red, but they're in
white, yellow, and black too.
Violets bloom in the cold so why
not embrace the chill too.
Flowers die so fruits can grow and
ripen as they naturally do.
And the world may be ugly, but it
can be beautiful for you.

Unload your burdens. Carry them with you.
Either way, you always have a choice.

www.ingramcontent.com/pod-product-compliance
Lightning Source LLC
Chambersburg PA
CBHW031239120626
46545CB00003B/1199